JN076691

アイルランド
IRELAND

人のいとなみ
LIFE AND PEOPLE

この本をアイルランドの人々に捧げます
To the people of Ireland

目次
Contents

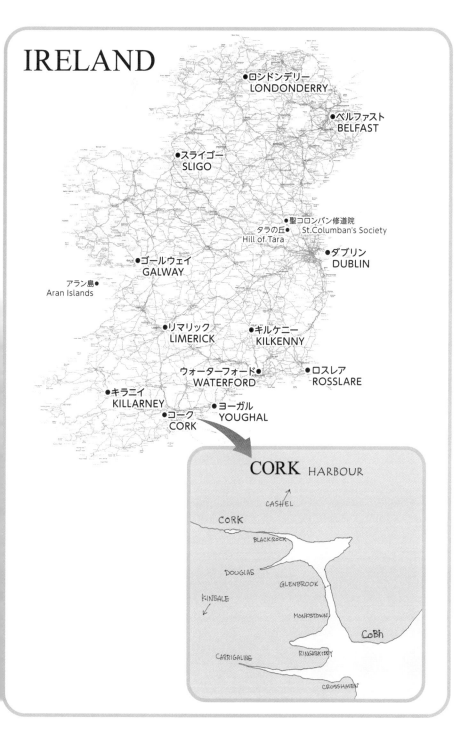

IRELAND

- ●ロンドンデリー LONDONDERRY
- ●ベルファスト BELFAST
- ●スライゴー SLIGO
- ●聖コロンバン修道院 St.Columban's Society
- タラの丘● Hill of Tara
- ●ダブリン DUBLIN
- ●ゴールウェイ GALWAY
- アラン島● Aran Islands
- ●リマリック LIMERICK
- ●キルケニー KILKENNY
- ウォーターフォード● WATERFORD
- ●ロスレア ROSSLARE
- ●キラニイ KILLARNEY
- ●コーク CORK
- ●ヨーガル YOUGHAL

CORK HARBOUR

- CASHEL
- CORK
- BLACKROCK
- DOUGLAS
- GLENBROOK
- KINSALE
- MONKSTOWN
- COBh
- CARRIGALINE
- RINGASKIDDY
- CROSSHAVEN

みどりの国　A GREEN COUNTRY

丘の眺め
A SOUTH CORK HILLSIDE

コーク南方

休日　　　　　　　　　　　　　　　　　　　　　　　　　キンセール
A WEEKEND NEAR KINSALE

…キミはこれからまだ旅が長いんだろう。おつりを少し多めにしておくよ。

アイルランドの田舎（カントリーサイド）をひとり旅していると、こんな場面にときどき出会うことがあります。

アイルランド（IRELAND）は漢字で愛蘭土と書きます。なんてかわいいのでしょう。実際に訪れてみるとアイ
ルランドの国土と人の営みはまさにそのような世界なのです。

Introduction

"You still have a long way to go. I will give you a lot of coins in the change." When I was
travelling alone through the countryside of Ireland, I met people who said things like that to
me.

The Chinese characters for Ireland traditionally used in Japan are 愛蘭土 . Don't they look
cute? When I visited Ireland and observed the landscape, the people and their activities, I
could see that they actually are as the characters suggest. 愛 means Love, 蘭 flower, and 土
Land.

緑の牧草地
PASTURELAND NEAR KINSALE

アイルランドは島国で日本の九州よりひとまわり大きなだ円形をしています。そして海の上にどらやきをそっと置いたように、全体が平らな高原状の地形です。すなわち海岸は急な立ち上がりの崖が多く、登ってしまえばやわらかな起伏がどこまでも続く緑の国です。「大西洋のエメラルド」の呼び名があります。この写真は春の夕刻で左からの傾いた陽差しがあたりをやさしく包んでくれています。ほかの国ではカメラを向けると怒り出す牛に

The island of Ireland is somewhat similar in shape to, and twice the size of the Japanese island of Kyushu. Like a small pancake sandwich quietly floating on water, there is a plateau-like aspect to the topography of the island as a whole. Along the coast cliffs rise sharply from the sea, and when one climbs over them, a soft undulating green landscape spreads over the island. Ireland is sometimes called the Emerald Isle of the Atlantic. In this photograph the evening

キンセール

出会ったことがありますが、ここでは特になにもなく、彼らはいつものように鼻先を草の中に入れていました。ひとりだけこちらを向いているけれど、このあとすぐにわれ関せずと食事に夢中になりました。「この国は嵐がほとんどないんだ」とジョンが教えてくれたことを思い出しました。

sunshine of Spring gently covers the fields as it spreads out from the left. In other countries I have met cattle which gave an angry look when I turned my camera towards them, but these paid me little heed, and mostly kept their noses focused on the green grass. One of them is looking toward me, but soon afterward decided to ignore me and continued to be absorbed in eating grass. I recalled that John told me that "there are few storms in this country."

リー川（北まわり）　　　　　　　　　　　　　　　　　　　　　　　　　　　　コーク
LOOKING AT THE NORTHSIDE OF CORK CITY

コークはアイルランド第2の都市。西から東にリー川が流れ市内で北と南の2つに分かれ、再び収束して海に向かいます。中洲の繁華街はほど良い広さで商店や飲食店それに Pub そしていくつかの教会が点在しています。

Cork is the second largest city in the Republic of Ireland. The river Lee flows from west to east through the city, where its two channels create an island which split the city into north and south before they converge again and head towards the sea. The centre city area features

ひこうき雲 コーブ
VAPORTRAIL OVER COBH

手ごろな料金のホテルも数多く一週間ほど、いやそれ以上の滞在も発見や楽しみの連続です。

a shopping district with wide footpaths and numerous cafes, restaurants and pubs, and is dotted with churches. I noticed that there are also many reasonably priced hotels, so one can stay for a week or more and enjoy the city.

コーブの港
CORK HARBOUR FROM COBH

コーブの港

タイタニック号のことを知っていてもこの港が最終寄港地であったことは日本ではあまり知られていません。
この画は丘の上の教会からのアングルですが中央の家並のいちばん先、山吹色に塗装された建物がそのころの
タイタニックの船会社・ホワイトスター社です。
イギリスのポーツマスを出港した船はこの港でアイルランドからの乗客をのせて大西洋に船出しました。アメリカ
大陸まであと少しのところで氷山に衝突・沈没したのですが、この時アイルランドの人びとも多数亡くなりました。

The town of Cobh

Even among those who have heard of the sinking of the Titanic, it is not widely known
that Cobh was her last port of call. The angle of my photograph of the harbour was at the
cathedral on the hill overlooking the town. The first house of the terrace, the building
painted yellow, was an office of the White Star Line, the owners of the Titanic. After leaving
Portsmouth, in England, the liners usually stopped at Cobh to take on Irish passengers, and
then set sail across the Atlantic. More than half way through her voyage the Titanic hit an
iceberg and sank, and many Irish people were also drowned. There is a museum about the

街にはタイタニック博物館があって往時を偲ぶ遺品が展示されています。
アイルランドの人びとが移民としてアメリカに渡ったことはよく知られているのですが、有名なケネディ大統領の曽祖父もそのひとりでした。また映画「風と共に去りぬ」のラストシーンで主人公スカーレットが「タラ」と小さくしかし力強く叫ぶ台詞がありますが、そのタラはアイルランド・ダブリン北方の聖地の名前です。高台の教会の鐘はどこまでも遠くまで響きます。
付）日本で有名な小泉八雲（ラフカディオ・ハーン）もアイルランド人です。

Titanic in Cobh, displaying various items commemorating the tragedy.
It is well know that many Irish people immigrated to the United States of America, and the famous President Kennedy was a descendent of one of them. In the last scene of Gone with the Wind the heroine, Scarlet says "Tara" in a low but strong voice. Tara is the ancient name of a sacred hill north of Dublin.
Lafcadio Hearn, well known as Koizumi Yakumo in Japan, was also of Irish descent.
The bells of Saint Coleman's cathedral can be heard over a wide are of the countryside.

郵便ポスト　　　　キンセール
POST BOX IN KINSALE

ラウンドアバウト（ロータリー）
THE FINGERPOST ROUNDABOUT IN DOUGLAS

ラウンドアバウト（ロータリー）はアイルランドの交差点では頻繁に出合います。信号がないので止まる必要が
なく、ゆっくり車を進めます。このラウンドアバウトは花がたくさん植えられていて、地元の人々が大切に愛おし

The roads in Ireland feature many rotaries or "roundabouts." There are usually no traffic
lights there, so one does not need to stop, and can proceed slowly, providing one gives way to
traffic coming from the right. Many flowers are in bloom at this roundabout in the suburb of

ダグラス

んでいる気持が伝わって来ます。方向板が示す先にそれぞれ指の絵があるので、ここは"フィンガーポスト"の愛称で呼ばれています。

Douglas, and I sense that the local people are proud of their home. The signpost has fingers pointing out the various roads, and is called the Fingerpost.

ハイクロス   ロックオブキャシェル

A CELTIC CROSS GRAVESTONE IN CASHEL

ケルト民族の十字架には太陽を表わす円が付与されています。
ロックオブキャシェルは平原の大きな岩の上に建立された修道院の遺跡です。あたりには牛や羊が放牧されて
いて、いかにもアイルランドらしい風景です。

The Celtic peoples often attach a circle – representing the sun – to their crosses. On the Rock of
Cashel, in county Tipperary, there remains the stone ruins of a church, cathedral and bishop's
residence. Green fields, with grazing cattle, surround the ruins – such a typical Irish scene.

山奥の修道院　　　　　　　　　　　　　　　グーガンバラ
THE LAKESIDE CHAPEL IN GOUGANE BARRA

妖精が住む山の中。細い道が一本だけ。
コーク市内から車で2時間ほど、道が細くなってクネクネと山を登ります。小さな湖と小さなチャペル、いまは
湖畔にホテルが一軒。巻頭のおじさんはここに来る途中で出会いました。

There is just one narrow road leading to the lake of Gougane Barra. Fairies are said to live among these hills. This beautiful and tranquil place is about two hours drive from Cork city, and the road zigzags for much of the way. There is a little stone chapel on the lakeside, and one small hotel nearby. Along the way I met an elderly man who gave me change (P.5).

河口の村
THE RIVER LEE AT PASSAGE WEST AND GLENBROOK

河口の村　グレンブロック

コークの街を流れて来たリー川はここグレンブロックでコーブの海に出ます。写真手前はコーブがわの岸、むこうはグレンブロックの集落です。川岸の道路に沿って小さなかわいい家が立ち並びます。

A riverside village : Glenbrook

After passing through the city of Cork, the river Lee flows alongside the village of Glenbrook before approaching Cobh and merging with the sea in Cork harbour. I took this photograph from the Cobh bank of the river, looking across at the village of Glenbrook. Terraces of mult

グレンブロック

この地が美しいのは水面、家並、そしてうねうねと連なる丘のおかげです。家々の並びや大きさ色彩などから
ここに住む人たちがこの地を大切にしていることが伝わって来ます。おだやかな水面とおだやかな稜線に包まれ
ておだやかな日々が過ぎて行きます。

coloured houses look out on to the river. The village houses spread out along the gentle slope
of the hills make this a most beautiful sight. The many colours of the rows of houses show
how much the people living here value their home. The calm river and calm waterfront offer
tranquil days for those who linger here.

17

アイルランドの国花　フクシア　　　　　シャンバリー教会
FUCHSIA AT SHANBALLY

シャンバリー教会では撮影したフィルムを無くしてしまいました。つめ替え作業で〝ちょっとそのへん〟に置いて忘れてしまいました。くやしいのでもう一度訪れた時にこのフクシアと出会いました。冷たい雨と風をものともせずに咲き続けています。
アイルランドの国の花。日本でも入手可能です。

I lost the film on which were my photographs of Shanbally church. When packing my belongings I placed it somewhere, and it disappeared. Annoyed, I visited the place again and came across this lovely fuchsia. It continues to bloom in spite of the cold wind and rain. This is one of the flowers of Ireland. It is also growing in Japan.

ひととき
RESTING ON THE RIVERSIDE

モンクスタウン
MONKSTOWN

汽水域で羽根を休める白鳥たち。そばに近づいても逃げない。
丘に立つ教会のふもとで昼食をとりました。入口は小さくても奥行は広くて、でも窓ぎわの小さな席に腰かけました。オーダーのあとひとしきり首を回すと、なんと、どこかの国と同じで、女性たちのグループがテーブルの大半を占めておしゃべりに夢中…！…

The swans are resting on the riverside. They do not move away as I approach. I ate my lunch in a restaurant at the foot of the hill going up to the church. The entrance is narrow, but inside is wide, and I sat on a chair at one of the windows. When I look around after ordering lunch, just as in any other country, at another table a group of women were absorbed in conversation.

夕宴のひととき
EVENING MEAL AT JOHN AND PHIL'S HOUSE IN CORK

夕宴のひととき
秋の明るい夕刻、僕のために晩餐を催してくれました。
お祈りのあと白ワインで乾盃。小さく言葉を交わしながらゆっくり静かに食べ始めたのですがカメラマンの欲求にブレーキをかけることができず、「ちょっと失礼」とこのショットをカシャリ。
出来上りのプリントを見るとミレーの晩鐘を思い出してしまいました。

A pleasant evening
It was a bright autumnal evening, and they had prepared a supper for me. After a prayer we toasted with white wine. Speaking softly, we began to eat, but the cameraman in me could not be contained, and saying "please excuse me" I captured the scene. Although the distant scene outside the window was a little blurred, it appeared to blend in with the table scene.

ジョンの家　コーク

窓のむこうの少しかすんでもやがかかった外気とはるか遠くに人の息吹き。
左のエドはひくい声で話しかけようとしている。
右のジョンはそれを受けながら皿に目を落として相づちをうつ。フィルも会話に参加しているけれど、あえて言葉は発しない。そのほうが祈りの食卓にふさわしいから。

When I looked at the printout it reminded me of Millet's The Angelus. Ed, on the left, is about so say something in a soft voice. John, on the right, is listening, and looking at his plate as he echoes Ed's words. Phil follows the conversation also, but does not venture to say anything. This suits the prayerful meal.

ボクはリー４才
I AM FOUR YEARS OLD

クロスヘブン
CROSSHAVEN

Lee　ボクは４才
４本の指をうまく開けない、
でもいっしょうけんめいポーズをとってくれる。
小馬にまたがってギッタンバッコンしながら
「I am pirate　ボクは海賊だ！」

Lee – I am four years old
He had difficulty opening out his four fingers, but he did his best to pose for me. He sat astride a little horse, and moving himself back and forth, shouted " I am a pirate."

22

ビディとライ
BIDDY AND RYNAGH IN THEIR HOUSE IN DOUGLAS

ビディの家　ダグラス

ビディからの手紙
A LETTER FROM BIDDY

Dear Tatsuya,

Thank you for the lovely postcards and gifts you sent me.

Wishing you and your family a happy and holy Christmas

hope to see you soon

Regards

Biddy McSweeney
The Fingerpost
Douglas

ライは毎週土曜日にこの家に来る。
いつも一緒に過ごす。
ビディは 50 年以上もここに住んでいる。小さな古い家だけれどア
イルランドではあたりまえ。室をきれいに飾って毎日をのんびり暮
らしている。日曜日には僕を教会につれていってくれた。巻頭の
飾り皿はこの家の廊下。

Rynagh visits mother in law, Biddy, every Saturday, and spends the afternoon with her.
Biddy has been living here for over 50 years. It is a small house, but not unusual in Ireland.
Biddy decorates her home carefully and likes living there. She took me with her to church on
Sunday. The ornamental plate at the front of this book is from the hallway of her house.

みんないっしょ
ALL TOGETHER

エドの家族
左から　ジェニファー，クローディ，
キャサリン，エド

JENNI,
CLODAGH, CATHLEEN,
EDDIE

リーの家族
左から　キャサリン，リー

LEE AND HIS FAMILY

デイブの家族
左から　リンダ，ジェシー，
デイブ，キャリー

LYNDA, JESS,
DAVID AND CARRIE

まくらもと
MY BEDSIDE

Lee のだいじだい
LEE'S IMPORTA
TOYS

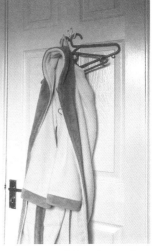

ベッドルームコーナー
BEDROOM DOOR

ドアのサイン
DOOR SIGN

Lee の木馬
LEE'S ROCKING HORSE

朝の光
THE MORNING SUN SHINING
INTO THE KITCHEN

キッチンのコーナー
A KITCHEN CORNER

毎日の生活
THE KITCHEN I USED
TO MAKE BREAKFAST

浴室
THE BATH

坂道
A QUIET STREET IN CORK CITY

コークの子どもたち。ただし撮影は 10 年以上も前。哲学を求める少年も。

School children around Cork city.
These photographs were taken over 10 years ago.

コーク

本屋のジョン　　　　　　　　　　　　　　　　　　　　　　　　　　　　　　　　　　ダグラス

A PORTRAIT OF JOHN O'LEARY

本屋のジョン

「もしトーキョーに行くことがあったらオペラを観たいなぁ」

ジョンは足繁くコークのオペラハウスに通っています。

あのソプラノの天を通りぬけるほどの声はまるでヒトのものとは信じ難いし、男声のあの低音も…、神様はど

John the Bookseller

"If I ever visit Tokyo I would like to go to the opera" he said to me. This John frequentl
attends the Cork opera house. The way that soprano's voice pierces the heavens makes it har
for you to think of her as human...the deep sound of that man. God really did make so man
different types of human beings.

むこうは海　　　　　　　　　　　Lee の家　クロスヘブン
A VIEW OF CROSSHAVEN FROM LEE'S HOUSE

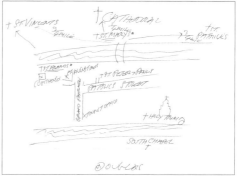

ジョンが説明してくれたコークの地図
ILLUSTRATION BY JOHN O'LEARY

やってこんなに多彩にヒトの体を作ったのだろう。

ジョンの会話はつねに知的でやさしい。ひとつひとつの言葉がていねいに吟味されているようだ。それを日本人の僕のためにゆっくり句切りながら。

窓ごしのやわらかい光とほおづえのポーズ、そこからにじみでる彼の人柄、そして沈黙のうちに醸し出される時。

My conversation with John was intelligent and pleasant. He pronounced each work politely and clearly for me, and spoke slowly so that I, as a Japanese, could understand what he said. He posed for me beside the window of his little bookshop just as the soft sunlight shone through. The scene seemed to capture his personality, as he relaxed into the silence.

ジョンとフィル   ジョンの家
JOHN AND PHIL AT HOME

Phil（フィル）は僕の英語の先生。といっても特にお願いしたわけでも、お金を払って契約したわけでもありません。けれど"そのいいかげんさをまったく意に介さない僕の英会話"の言葉の端しばしを上手に直してくれます。ほんの少しのアドバイスだけれどこれが日本での中学・高校の教科書のなん十倍もの効果てきめんで、なるほど百聞は一見にしかず、いや聞くと話すとの違い、それも実際の生活の中でのことなのでその呑み込みのいいこと、これがほんとの英語教室なのですね。

Some Irish Friends

Phil became my English teacher. I did not actually request her to do this, nor did I make an agreement and pay her money. But she politely corrected my poor English, although I did not care too much myself about the way I used the English words I knew. She only provided me with a little advice. But it was about ten times more effective than a Japanese Middle or High School textbook, and just as it is better to see something once than to hear about it one hundred times, I realised the difference between hearing and speaking English, and

窓打つ雨　　　　　　　　　　　　　　　　　　　　　　　ジョンの家
A WINDOW IN JOHN'S HOUSE ON A RAINY DAY

ちょうど来ていた Phil のお母さんが昔の唄を僕に歌ってくれました。2、3 曲。知っているのもあったので大き
な拍手をみんなで送りました。ありがとう。
John は最近この家を建てました。
ガレージの半分はクラフト工房になっていて、彼は材木を削り出して小さな家具やら食器やらを趣味で作ってい
ます。日本風に言えば高さ 10cmほどの茶筒を僕は帰りぎわにもらいました。日本に帰って来てから「なにかに

understood how words are used in everyday life. This was a true English class.
Phil's mother visited while I was there and taught me some old Irish songs. We gave her a
bigclap. Thank you.
John, Phil's husband, had recently been working on their house. Part of his garage was used
as a workshop, and with his woodturning he had made small pieces of furniture and food
bowls. When I was leaving he presented me with what in Japan would be a 10 centimetre
high tea canister. After returning to Japan, while wondering how I would use it, placed it on a

35

書斎　　　　　　　　　　　　　　　　　　　　　　　　ジョンの家

DINING ROOM TABLE USED AS A DESK WHEN JOHN WORKED AT HOME

ゲストルーム　　　　　　　　　　　　　　　　　　　　　ジョンの家
THE GUEST BEDROOM IN JOHN'S HOUSE

使おう」と棚の上にちょこんと置いたのですが、そのまま 10 年以上、今はそこの主になっています。
彼は休みの午後にはいつも広い広い庭の芝刈りをすることにしていて、専用の芝刈りバイクにまたがって正方形
の庭を 1 時間くらいかけて走り回ります。エンジンの音がギシギシと、なにやらミニトラクターのよう。
庭のむこうはゆるい谷になっていてさらにそのむこうに夕陽が落ちて行きます。

shelf, and it has remained there for the past 10 years. John often spends an afternoon cutting
the grass in his large garden, riding a tractor mower back and forth for an hour. The sound of
the engine reminded me of a mini tractor. The distant part of his garden gently descends into
a valley, and the evening sun sinks away over it.

37

ディスプレイ
LIVINGROOM DISPLAY

ひとり住まいをさせてもらったこの家は以前はお店屋さんだったそうです。家族は敬虔なカトリック信者でした。アイルランドでは住まいのコーナーや階段などにマリア像や小さなイエス様の像が置いてあります。P.52 や目次ページの小さなマリア像などがそれです。日本では宗教はあまり重要視されていませんが、この地では日々の生

The house where I stayed on my own had once been a grocery shop. The family were devout Catholics. In a corner of Irish homes or in a hallway or staircase there is often a staute of Our Lady or Our Lord, and there were some here also. The small statue of Our Lady on the Contents page of this book is one of these. In Japan there are few such displays of religious devotion, but in Ireland one observes that for many people daily life is often based on

ダグラス

活すべてが信仰に基づいています。日曜の礼拝はもちろんですが、毎日正午と午後6時になるとテレビやラジオから鐘の音が流れます。みんな手を休めてしばしの安らぎと共に祈りをささげます。写真は以前この家に住んでいたウィリアムとキャサリン夫妻です。

religious faith. They go to church to worship on Sundays, and at 12 noon and 6PM each day the Angelus bell can be heard on the radio and television. At these times many people join their hands and offer a prayer during a tranquil moment. This display contains pictures of William and Catherine O'Driscoll, who once lived where I stayed.

キッチン　エドの家

三脚を置き忘れた話

教会の庭に三脚を置き忘れた、と気付いたのは翌日の朝。いつも置いているクルマの後部座席にそれが見当らなくて、トランクを開けたり床を探したり、「もしかしたら家の中に入れたかも」と思って部屋じゅう2回も見まわったりしたのですが、どうにも見つからないのです。

アナログカメラ時代にきちんとした画像を撮るための三脚は必須条件で、屋外の撮影なら手持ちでなんとかなるのですが暗い教会の内部や民家の室内ではカメラを固定してブレないようにするためにどうしても三脚がなければなりません。

この先まだ数日、数ヶ所の撮影予定があるのにどうしようと絶望に打ちひしがれて、それでも「もしかして」と思い現地に行ってみたところ、ない。そこにはなかったのでした。

がっかりして John に電話すると「教会に行って神父様に聞いてみたら」と。でも僕の頭の中には海外旅行＝盗難に気をつけろ、のじゅ文がこびり着いていたので"そんなのある筈ないよね"と。それでも近くに住むもうひ

The day I forgot my tripod

It was the following morning when I realised that I had left my tripod in the church garden. I could not find it on the back seat of the car where I usually left it. I opened the boot and looked inside, and then thought "maybe I left it in my living room." I had twice looked around my room, and there was no sign of it there either.

During the era of the analogue camera a tripod was essential for taking a clear image. When taking shots outside I could somehow manage holding the camera in my hand, but when taking photographs in the dark interior of a church or inside the room of a family dwelling, in order to fix the position of the camera and prevent it shaking, a tripod is essential. Since I had planned to take photographs in a number of places during the coming days I was giving way to despair when I thought "perhaps..." and went to look at a place I had been, but there was no sign of it. It was not there. Disappointed, I telephoned John, and he suggested that I go to the church and ask the priest about the missing tripod. But inside me were the warnings

キッチン Lee の家
KITCHEN SCENES IN LEE'S HOME

キッチン ジョンの家
KITCHEN SCENE IN JOHN'S HOME

とりの John に「きのう三脚を教会に忘れた」と相談に（というより告げに）行くと「神父様に聞いてみたら」と同じ返事。気を静めるためにいったん部屋に戻って昼ごはんを食べていると "この国ってそういう国なのかい?" と心の中にすこし希望が見えてきました。

ふたりの John に同じことを言われて教会に行かないわけにもいかないので、午後になって半信半疑のまま歩を進めました。

神父様はなぜか教会の外で信徒と立ち話をしていたので僕は近寄って「きのう三脚を置き忘れたのですが」と伝えるとすぐさま「ほらここにあるよ、君のだろう」と司祭館の玄関の中を指差したのでした。

"えっアイルランドってこういう国なの" 僕はなんだかテレビのドラマの中にいるような自分をそこに発見したのでした。ここでも神父様や信徒の人たちはやっぱりニコニコ、お礼もそこそこに 2 人の John に報告すると、またまた口を揃えたように「ほらね、よかったね」。

about being on the alert for thieves when travelling abroad, and I did not think it could be found. But when I asked another man called John who lived beside where I was staying, he also said "why not go and ask the priest." As I returned to my room to eat lunch and try and settle my feelings, I thought "maybe this country is that kind of country" and a little hope began to arise within me. Since the two Johns had told me the same thing, I could not but go back to the church, and so in the afternoon, half in doubt, I made my way back to the church. The priest was standing outside the church talking to one of the parishioners as I approached him. When I told him "yesterday I left a tripod around here" he immediately replied "I have it here, it must be yours," and pointed to a spot inside the entrance of his house. "Ah, this is Ireland" I thought to myself, and felt like I was discovering myself in a television drama. The priest and his parishioner smiled as I left. When I told the two Johns later that I had recovered the tripod they both replied "there you are, what did I tell you?"

ジェニファー
JENNI

クローディとイヌのキャシー
CLODAGH AND CASSIE

おめでとう　　　　　　　　　　　　　　　　　　　　　コーク大学　ホーナンチャペル

A WEDDING SCENE AT THE HONAN CHAPEL IN UNIVERSITY COLLEGE CORK

ソーダブレッドをスーパーで買い求める

フィンガーポスト（と呼ばれている家＝彼の地では建物や家に名前がつけられていることも多い）にはじめて泊った時知らずに口にしたのがソーダブレッド。日本ではほとんどお目にかからないけれどこれが得も言われぬ絶妙な味、舌ざわり、香りなのです。口の中で咬めばかむほどにその香りが腔内（口の中）を満たし「これはなに!?!」と目がパッチリほっぺがついゆるんでしまう、僕にはそんな存在なのです。

ひとり暮しだったので徒歩５分のスーパーに買い出しに行った時、パンの売場で初老のカップルといっしょになっ

Buying Soda Bread in a supermarket

The first piece of food I placed in the mouth, when I stayed at a house near the Fingerpost, in Douglas, a suburb of Cork, unknowingly, was soda bread. This type of bread is rarely seen in Japan, and has a rather delicate fine taste and smell. When you chew it the flavour fills your mouth, your eyes open wide, your cheeks relax – that is what I experienced.

44

リー川と好ましい建物たち（北まわり）　　　　　　　　　　　　　　　　　コーク
A QUAYSIDE IN CORK

たのですが例によって「日本からなにしに来てるの？」なんて始まって多くの種類のパンの中から「どれがソー
ダブレッドですか？」と尋ねると急にニコニコしてこう教えてくれるのでした。
「ソーダブレッドはこの国では昔からのものなんだ。みんな大好きだよ」と我が意を得たとばかりの解説が口か
らポンポンと出て来ました。「こっちの銘柄が美味しいわよ」なんて奥さんも。値段は 1.5 ユーロ≒ 200 円くらい。
ひとつ買うとこれで 2 〜 3 日はなんとか過ごせます。ソーダブレッドはふつうのパンよりも発酵が進み易いので

I was staying there on my own, and when I went to buy some at a supermarket about five
minutes walk away, there was an elderly couple in front of me in the queue. When I saw
many different types of bread, I asked them "which is soda bread?" They smiled as they
pointed it out to me. "Soda bread has been made here for a long time. Everybody likes it,"
they said, as if knowing what I was thinking. "This type is delicious" the wife added.

セントメリー教会　リー川（北まわり）　　　　　コーク
ST.MARY'S CHURCH, CORK

CORK CITY

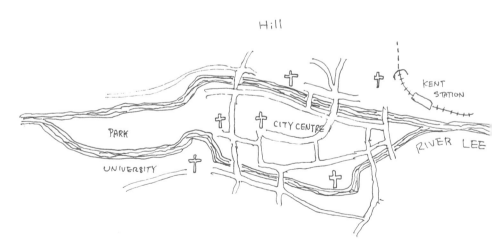

もうすぐ夕方　セントフィンバラス教会　リー川 (南まわり)　　　　　　コーク
ST.FIN BARR'S CATHEDRAL

暖かい季節ではすぐに食べてしまわなければなりません。このごろは London のコンビニでも売っているけれど、賞味期限はたいがい１～２日以内となっているので購入したらすぐさまひたすらもぐもぐと毎食それをノルマ化する必要に迫られます。
しかしここアイルランドの秋から冬はそんなことちっとも気にすることなしに、台所のそのへんに置きっぱなしで特に問題にはなりません。もっとも問題にしていないのは僕ひとりのつごうだけで、少しずつは変化しているの

The price was 1.5 euro (about 200 Yen). If I buy one, it will last for two or three days, I thought to myself.
Soda bread ferments easily, and must be eaten soon during the hot season. These days it is even on sale in convenience stores in London, and the label says it stays fresh for about two days. Normally it appears necessary to eat it fresh after purchase.

夕やけのころ　リー川（北まわり）
SUNSET OVER THE NORTHSIDE OF CORK CITY

だろうけれど味オンチの僕はそんなことお構いなしに数日間マイペースでそれを楽しみながら撮影の日々を送る
のでした。
その味は実に芳醇で、なぜかなつかしい香りが舌と心を癒やしてくれるような、そんなやさしさが伝わってくる
のです。

But during autumn and winter in Ireland there seems to be no need to worry about this, and
it can be left around in the kitchen for a few days. I never bother too much about freshness
dates and such like, so I just enjoyed eating soda bread at my own pace during the days I was
travelling around taking photographs.
Soda bread certainly has a sweet taste, and the strangely nostalgic and gentle taste heals both

コーク

ですから彼の地では常にそれを買い求めるのですが、だれか日本でも製品化してくれませんか。
口の中でボロボロと崩れていくその嚙みごこちと心の温もりを、ぜひ日本の食卓へ!!

my tongue and my heart. I often bought soda bread while in Ireland, and wondered if anyone
in Japan would begin baking it for sale. The taste of soda bread dissolving in my mouth and
the warm feeling this evokes in my heart is something I would like to bring to the Japanese
dining table.

河口の村
THE RIVER LEE AT GLENBROOK

グレンブロックのフェリー GLENBROOK FERRY
この岸の間には乗船時間3分のフェリーボートが往復しています。船の形は平らな板の中央にちょこんと運転室がある簡単なもので両方向に進みます。

上から見た図 よこから見た図

グレンブロック

甲板上にキップを売るおじさんがいて、クルマで乗り込むと窓ごしに "oneway?"（片道）と聞くので "Return"（往復）と答えると割引キップにしてくれました。3ユーロ（440円くらい）だったかな。時刻表なんてなくて、クルマが集まるとてきとうに発車、いや出港します。ここに橋を架けない理由はこの美しい景色をこわさないため？

The Glenbrook Ferry crosses the river Lee in just a few minutes. The ferryboat is of a flat surface, with a small cabin at the centre of one side for the pilot and pedestrian passengers. Vehicles can enter and leave at both ends. A crew member sells tickets to the drivers of the cars, asking if they require a single, a return, or a discounted batch of tickets. I purchased the discounted batch for 3 euro – about 440 Yen. There was no timetable to be seen, and as soon as the cars were on the ferry it started off across the river. Perhaps the reason they do not build a bridge here is because it will spoil the scenery?

祈りとやすらぎ
PRAYER AND TRANQUILITY

御聖体ランプ　　　　　　　　　　　　　　ダグラス
ELECTRIC LAMP BEFORE
A PICTURE OF THE HOLY FAMILY

聖堂とルルドの洞窟　　　　　　　　　クロスヘブン教会
GROTTO AND CHURCH　　ST.BRIGID'S CHURCH IN CROSSHAVEN

祈りと安息

「質素な生活なんでしょう、アイルランドの人たちって」と僕がアイルランドを訪れたことを知って、日本人はみんな口を揃えてこう言います。「ぜぇーんぜん！日本より豊か」と僕は答えます。お金や国の力のことは解らないけれどひとりのふつうの人として見る限り、

Prayer and Rest

Japanese people who know that I have visited Ireland always say "Their life is a simple life – the people of Ireland." But I always reply "Not at all ! They are wealthier than Japanese."I do not know about the financial wealth

丘の教会
CROSSHAVEN

彼らの方が日本人よりよほど余裕が見られます。

心のゆとりというのか生活のテンポというのか、たぶん日本よりもゆっくりしていると思われます。たとえばカフェに座り込みビール一杯で一時間も会話をつないでいる人たち、彼らはとりとめのない冗談を言い合っていることもあるけれど、耳をそば立ててみるとなにやら深い意味の社会性のある会話をしているようにも聞こえます。それもいっしょうけんめい。

日本ではこんな時あたりさわりのない言葉使いでその場をまるく収めるというかやり過ごすことが多いのですが彼らはどうやらそうではなさそうです。まるで重箱の隅をつっつくかのような細かいところまで確認をし合っているようにも見受けられるのです。

大げさに言えば深い意味の合意とでも形容しましょうか。なるほど、この国は、ひとつのことにこんなに多くの時間をかけられる社会なんだと、そんなところからも人々の生活と心の豊かさを発見してしまうのです。

さらに几帳面な日本人（僕はそうではないけれど）からするとかなり大ざっぱなところもあって、それが僕から見るとゆとり・包容力というふうに思えるのです。たとえば日本にはガイジン(外国人)という言葉があるけれどアイルランドやヨーロッパにはそういう単語は無いのではないかと思われるのです。その理由はロンドンやダブリンの街を歩いているとそれはそれはいろいろな人種の人がふつうにたくさんたくさん歩いているからです。日本の高校のように生徒の髪の毛の色をいちいち気にしていることはないのです。

それらはすでに当然のこととして社会のコンセンサスがなん百年

クロスヘブン教会

and the strength of the country, but just looking at ordinary people, I feel that they have so much more than Japanese people.

It maybe the comforts they enjoy, or the pace of their lives. I think they live at a slower pace than Japanese.

For example there are people who sit around a table in a cafe or pub and spend an hour talking over a glass of beer; they talk in a rambling manner and tell each other jokes; but listening closely I get the feeling that there is some deep social contact there in that conversation. And they are seriously communicating with each other.

In Japan there are many times we enjoy harmless conversation and the companionship such occasions provide, but somehow among the Irish this seems to be different. It appears as if they are delicately probing a tiered box and seeing what is inside as they affirm their relationships. If I may exaggerate a little, these gatherings may be a metaphor for agreement on some deep meaning. Ireland is a country which spends a lot of time on this one practice, and it is here that one can gain insight into the richness of people's lives and hearts.

From a Japanese person's perfectionist point of view (I am not one) the Irish may often appear quite casual about things, but I see this as their being relaxed and

ステンドグラス　　　　　　　　　　　　　　　　　　　　　モンクスタウン教会
STAINED GLASS WINDOW IN MONKSTOWN CHURCH

も以前から成り立っているからです。
そのぶん細かいことにいちいち目クジラを立てないので、彼らはいつもニコニコ心豊かにいられるのです。
ただしなにをしてもいいということではなく、ひとりの市民・ひとりの大人として社会から要求される人格と社会

broad-minded. For example in Japan we have the word "gaijin" for foreigners, but in Ireland and Europe there is not an actually equivalent word. When you walk the streets of London or Dublin you normally see many people of various nationalities. People do not take notice of each and every different type of hairstyle and color like Japanese high school students problem. This is because there has been a social consensus formed hundreds of years ago that this is

聖マリア像と御聖体の火　　　　　　聖コロンバン修道院
OUR LADY'S ALTAR
AT ST.COLUMBAN'S CHAPEL IN COUNTRY MEATH

的要素は日本以上に大きな意味があります。

something normal. So they do not glare at such trifles, and just smile from the richness of their hearts. This does not mean that one may do anything, but that as a city dweller and as an adult there is a greater personality and consistency demanded by society that would be the case in Japan.

聖コロンバン修道院
ST.COLUMBAN'S, DALGAN PARK, NAVAN

２階の角部屋に泊めてもらった。辺りはなだらかに続く低い丘で、牛が草を噛む。天国のよう。

I stayed in a corner room on the first floor of Saint Columbans – a former training college for priests of the Missionary Society of Saint Columban. Surrounded by gently sloping green

ナーバン

日本での伝道を終えた数名の神父様とお茶や食事。

fields, with cows quitely grazing, it was like Heaven. There I drank tea and took my meals with some Catholic priests who had spent many years working in Japan.

ホーリートゥリニティ教会と修道院
HOLY TRINITY CHURCH AND FRANCISCAN HOUSE IN CORK ON

小雨のあと、虹のアーチが教会の尖塔に。

After rainfall, a rainbow arch touches the spire.

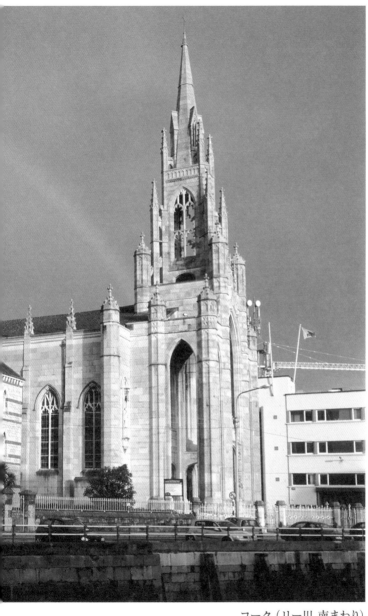

コーク（リー川 南まわり）

TH CHANNEL OF THE RIVER LEE

リタイアした機関長とコーブ大聖堂
COBH CATHEDRAL

コーブ・セントコールマンカテドラルと煙草のおじさん
「6年前にタバコをやめてね、今年からまた吸い始めたんだ」
もと遠洋航海船機関士のおじさんはそう言ってポーズをとってくれました。
「オレんちはあの坂の上で今はもう退職したからカミさんと2人でのんびりの毎日

Saint Coleman's Cathedral, Cobh, and the smoking man
"I gave up smoking six years ago, and started up again this year," a
former engineer of ocean-going ships said to me, as he posed for a
photograph.
"I am now retired and living a quiet life with my wife on top of

聖堂内見上げ　船底天井
HIGH ALTAR IN ST.COLEMAN'S CATHEDRAL, COBH

だよ」
「あっちのベンチにはいつもの仲間が大勢集って例によって世間話だよ。おじさんたちだってけっこうペチャク
チャやるんだぜ。タバコの煙がみんなの顔をすすけさせると困るのでひとりでこっちに来ているんだ」
ここは港の桟橋。入江には小舟が繋がれて暖かな波の動きに身を任せています。丘の上からは立派な教会が

hat hill… On that bench over there many of my friends gather, and we chat about life. They
chatter a lot, these old men. The tobacco smoke dries up their face, so I have to come over
here when I want a smoke."
We were standing at the landing pier. Around the inlet little boats were tied up and resting
themselves on the movement of the warm waves. On top of the hill a magnificent church was

祈り　　　　　　　　　　　　　　　　グーガンバラ修道院
PRAYER　　　　　　　　　　　　GOUGANE BARRA CHAPEL

この街とそこに住む人を見守ってまるでここはひとつの理想郷。
この写真は後日、届けに出向いた。本人は見当たらなかったけれどベンチのおじさん
にそれとなく見せると、ふたつ返事で " ああ、渡しておくよ "。

overlooking the town and its people, just as in some ideal setting.
St.Coleman's cathedral overlooks the town and its people – an ideal
setting. While I really did not aim to do so, when I showed the photo to
a man outside, he said "I will pass it on to him."

クリスマスの馬小屋
CHRISTMAS CRIB AT
ST.PATRICK'S CHURCH, CORK

セントパトリック教会　コーク

瞑想 カリガライン教会

STATUE OF SAINT JOSEPH IN CARRIGALINE CHURCH

鐘楼　　　　　　　　　　　　　　　　　　カリガライン教会
THE BELL AT CARRIGALINE CHURCH

被昇天のマリア様
MOSAIC OF THE ASSUMPTION OF OUR LADY IN CARRIGALINE CHURCH

カリガライン教会

雲にのって空の上をめざすこの姿は被昇天のマリア様と呼ばれます。
地上での行いを終え、帰天する姿です。
この日は毎年8月15日とされています。（モザイク画）

Standing on a cloud, facing and pointing toward Heaven, this mosaic
is a portrait of the Assumption of Our Lady into Heaven. Her life on
earth is complete, and she is being taken up into Heaven. The Feast
of the Assumption of Our Lady is on August 15th each year.

コークの中心部にそびえ立っている。
各々の教会には聖人の名を冠しているが、
ここでは聖ピーター（ペトロ）と聖ポール（パウロ）の2人の名がつけられている。

Saints Peter and Paul's church stands in a side street off the centre of
Cork city. Most churches are dedicated to some saint, and this one is
dedicated to two great saints Peter and Paul.

ピーターアンドポール教会　　　　　　　　コーク
ST.PETER AND PAUL'S CHURCH, CORK CITY

71

結婚式　　　　　　　　　　　　　　　ブラックロック教会
WEDDING FLOWERS AT BLACKROCK CHURCH

きれいな花々はあしたの結婚式の準備が終わったところ。
肺を患った女性とミニ会話。
「このあいだ肺ガンをやったの」「手術をしたのですか」
「そうよ。今はもうなんでもないわ」「無理しないでね…」

Preparations for the next day's wedding ceremony were just finished, and Blackrock church is decorated with flowers of many colours. I chatted briefly with an elderly lady who had lung disease: "I recently had an operation for lung cancer" she told me. "Did you really" I replied. "Yes" she responded, "and now I am fine." "Do not overdo it" I said.

しずか

聖フランシス教会

OUR LADY'S ALTAR IN ST.FRANCIS CHURCH

天使とともに登っていく
被昇天のマリア様
祈る人は心の安らぎ

Our Lady rises up with the angels toward Heaven. The Assumption of Our Lady comforts those who pray to her.

修道院
AN OLD CONVENT BUILDING IN KINSALE

まちと港を見おろす丘にあった古い修道院。

An old convent building overlooking the town and harbour.

キンセール
KINSALE

この撮影の時すでにひと気はなく、そして次に訪れた時はとり壊されて。

I did not have much time when I took this photograph, and when I visited the place again later the building had been demolished.

ひとり
INSIDE RINGASKIDDY ORATORY

YOKOSO
STATUE OF JESUS
OUTSIDE RINGASKIDDY ORATORY

リンガスキディ教会

YOKOSO
コークの街には2つの港がある。ひとつはタイタニック号が出港したコーブ（CoBh）の港、もうひとつはイギリス・ウェルズやフランスからのフェリーが到着するリンガスキディ（Ringaskiddy）港。
上陸すると正面にこの像と教会があって来訪者をむかえてくれる。
ほかでは見ることのできないイエス・キリスト像。

The Ringaskiddy Welcome
There are two harbours at the city of Cork. One of them is Cobh, which was the last stop of the Titanic, and the other is Ringaskiddy, where ferries from England, Wales and France berth. On the main street of Ringaskiddy, welcoming visitors, is a large statue of Christ holding a cross, of a kind not seen elsewhere.

リンガスキディ教会

雨あがり
ST.COLUMBA'S CHURCH DOUGLAS, CORK

雨上り（ダグラス教会）
となりに住むビディはもうなん十年もこの街に住んでいます。日ようの朝僕を礼拝につれていってくれました。そして神父様に引き合わせて撮影の許可をとってくれたのです。「日本のミサは静かすぎてまるでお葬式のようだ」と在日の外国人神父様たちは冗談めいて話しますが、ここアイルランドではなんと熱気があるのでしょう。ダグラスの教会は 2 ～ 300 人ほどがあつまるのですが、その聖堂の中はみんなの気持と精神の高揚でいっぱいです。だれも声は発しないけれどそれは僕のようなのほほんとした東洋人にもひしひしといやびりびりと伝わって来るようで、その力がどこから発せられているのか思わずあたりをキョロキョロとしてしまいました。
儒教仏教がなん千年にもわたって社会に浸透している日本を静とするとキリスト教や革命による社会の欧米は

After rainfall – Douglas Church
The woman who lived beside the house in which I was staying was named Biddy (short for Bridget) and had been living in Douglas for almost 50 years. She brought me to morning Mass, and got permission from the priest for me to take some photographs. Some foreign priests working in Japan had told me that Masses in Japanese churches were very quiet, and jokingly said they were almost like a funeral. In Ireland I felt that there was some enthusiasm among those who attended Mass. Two or three hundred people attend Sunday Mass each week in Douglas church, (the patron of the church is Saint Columba) and the church is filled with their feeling and spirit, although nobody raises

聖コロンバ教会（ダグラス）

聖堂内部
INSIDE ST.COLUMBA'S CHURCH

動と対比されます。どちらが良いかということではなく、これはそこに住む人々の伝統的な相異なのだと思われるのです。たとえばチョウにいろいろな種類があって好みの花のミツがそれぞれちがうように、ユーラシア大陸の東のはしと西のはしで同じはずがないのです。「伝統的なんだからそれはそれでいいんだ」と、日本ではあまり言いませんが彼の地では「Traditional（伝統的）だから」と言うとすべてを納得してもらえます。

そんなことを考えながら外に出ると先ほどまでの雨が止んでうっすらと青空がみえるようになりました。冬の風は冷たいけれど今日はなぜか爽やか。空気がまだ湿っているのでピリピリしないのです。

教会の墓地でカメラを構えていると中年の御婦人との会話になりました。

「僕は仏教ですが」

heir voice during Mass. As an agreeable Asian this church atmosphere clings to me intensely, and I cannot but look around and wonder where its strength comes from.

Over a period of almost a thousand years Buddhism filtered quietly into Japan, and can be contrasted with the entrance of Christianity and the revolutionary westernization of Japanese society. It is not the case that one is better than the other, but rather the traditional differences of the people involved.

Just there there are many types of butterfly and they each like a different kind of honey, so the eastern edge of the Eurasia continent cannot be the same as the western edge. In Japan we do not say things like "that is their tradition so it is alright," but here when someone says "it is traditional" everyone

雨の墓地
THE CATHOLIC GRAVEYARD IN DOUGLAS

「私はカトリックだけれど宗教はなんでもいいの、みんなが楽しく平和を愛して過ごせるなら宗教なんてなんでもいいの」
アイルランドは歴史的に他の国から多くの迫害を受けた経験がある国なので、この婦人の言葉からは格別の意味と重みを感じるのでした。

agrees with what is taking place.
As I was thinking like this I went outside and the rain which was falling earlier had stopped, and a blue sky began to slowly appear. The winter breeze was cold, but that day was somehow mild. The air was still moist, and felt soft.
When I was arranging my camera in the nearby graveyard, I got into conversation with a middle-aged lady. When I said "I am Buddhist" she replied "I am Catholic but I think every religion is alright

ダグラス　子どものおはか
A CHILD'S GRAVE

生まれて8ヶ月あまりで天国に逝ってしまった。
パパとママはいつも忘れないよ。

日本が朝鮮半島や中国を占領したようにアイルランドもローマ人やイギリス人による占領と宗教的な弾圧を受けました。
韓国の人が現在でも日本を非難し続けるのは歴史を忘れないためです。自分の国を占領されたことのない日本人はその心をほんとうに理解することができるのでしょうか。

and if people can live together happily and peacefully then any religion is fine." Ireland is a country which historically has suffered much damage from another country, and so I felt a special and particular meaning from this lady's words. Just as Japan colonised the Korean peninsula and China, Ireland was colonised by England and suffered religious persecution. Korean people still continue to criticise Japan because they cannot forget their history. Japan has never been colonised and so I wonder if Japanese people can really understand the feelings of those peoples whose countries were.

教会への道　　　　　　　　　　　　　　聖コロンバ教会（ダグラス）
ST.COLUMBA'S CHURCH DOUGLAS

よく踏み固められた土の道
ときどき手入れされている左右のみどり
午後の陽に並木が小さな影を
なん回も通って　なん枚も撮影
大好きなところだから。

The pathway has been hardened by the steps of many feet, the grass alongside is regularly trimmed. The trees cast a short shadow in the evening sunshine. I visited here a number of times and took many photographs – one of my favourite scenes.

今日もありがとう　　　　　　　　　　　　　　　　　　　　ダグラス
TWILIGHT AT ST.COLUMBA'S CHURCH, DOUGLAS

三脚をたたんでの帰り道
ふり返ると空が叫んでいる
鐘楼がなにごとかを語りかける
この街での最後のシャッターを。

set up again the tripod on my way home for this shot. It seems as if the sky is calling to me.
The bell rings, and sounds as if it too is saying something. I press the shutter for my final
photograph of this place.

抱よう
THE ROCK OF CASHEL

大きな岩の上の修道院。風もなく横からのおだやかな光。

The ruins of a church on top of a hill. There is no breeze, and soft light from the side.

ロックオブキャシェル

だれもいない広い牧草地。あたりは静か。

A couple alone in the large pasture. Nor is there any sound.

感謝　　　　　　　　　　　　　　　　　　グーガンバラ修道院
CROSS AT GOUGANE BARRA

あとがき　AFTERWORD

黒ビールのギネスは有名だけれどこのマーフィーズも爽やかで飲みやすい。取材中の心の友。
GUINNESS BLACK BEER (STOUT) IS FAMOUS, BUT MURPHY'S STOUT HAS A
SMOOTH TASTE AND IS EASY TO DRINK. MURPHY'S BECAME AN INTIMATE
FRIEND OF MINE DURING MY STAY IN IRELAND.

ミサの熱

アイルランドで数回ミサに与りました。信徒たちのエネルギーはすさまじいもので、となりに座っている人の熱気が直接伝わって来るのです。肩と肩が触れ合っているわけでもなく会話を交すわけでもないのですが、人々の眼差しや物腰から熱い思いを感じてしまうのです。聖体拝領（神父様から各自がパンをもらう）の時にもわれ先に椅子を立ち祭壇をめざします。まるで神様に吸い寄せられるように。その時は人々の足音や動き回る仕草の音が聖堂を大きく揺らします。日本での静かなミサに慣れているのではじめのうちはこのちがいにびっくりす

Attending Mass

I attended Mass a number of times in Ireland. The spirit of Irish Catholics is marvellous, and I could feel the devotion of the people around me. We were not standing shoulder to shoulder, nor were we conversing with one another, but I felt a warm intensity emanating from their expressions and from their manner. When receiving Holy Communion (a small round piece of bread transformed into spiritual nourishment) from the priest, they move intentionally from their seats toward the altar, just as if they were drawn there by Almighty God. During

コーク市内うら通りの窓辺。アイルランドでは外から見えるようにマリア様を置く家も多い。
A WINDOW SILL ON THE SIDE OF A STREET IN CORK CITY. MANY HOMES PLACE
A STATUE OF OUR LADY AT THEIR WINDOWS SO IT MAY BE SEEN BY PASSERS-BY.

ることばかりでしたが、なるほどこれが「本来の自発的なミサなのだ」と理解するようになりました。
言葉が適切でないかも知れませんが、古くからの儒教の色あいが濃い日本社会では上から下へのベクトルが強
く、カトリックのミサでも神父様→信徒の方向が厳守されています。ところがこの国ではベクトルの方向が信徒

that time the sound of peoples' footsteps and the movement of their bodies echoes throughout
the church. Since I am used to much more stillness at Masses in Japan, I was at first surprised
by such manner of movement, but I soon came to realise that this was quite a normal aspect
of the Mass. My manner of expression may not be appropriate, but in Japan, where there has
been a strong religious consciousness since ancient times, and the top down vector is strong,
during the Catholic Mass the practice of priest and people facing each other is strictly
adhered to. So here I did not sense a vector of people facing Almighty God, but rather one

→神のように思われてなりません。人々は神様にお願い
するのではなく、自己の主体と共に神が存在する、また
は自分を実現、成就するために神と共に歩むといった生
命倫理に基づく自然の行動を具現しているのではないか
と思わざるを得ないのです。カトリックという言葉は日
本語で「公」とされます。この場合の公は日本で言うと
ころのおカミ・権力者という意味ではなく、日常の不偏
のもの・そこにあるふつうの営み・あたりまえ、といっ
た言葉での表現があてはまるように思えます。ここでも
やはりベクトルの方向が相対しています。そういえば民
主主義の原点であるフランス革命のベクトルはやはり市
民→権力者だったわけで、人々の日々の営みもそしてカ
トリックの意味もここに重なるものと思えるのです。静
かな日本のミサ（冗談で「お葬式のよう」と外国人神父
様方はたとえます……）でそれを「もの足りないな」と
思っている人々がいます。フィリピンの人たちです。佐
渡の教会で出会った彼らは古いタタミの上でミサの最中
に歌って踊ります。ちょっと押さえ気味にトーンダウンし
ているようですが、本国ではもっと楽しそうにやってい
たのでしょうね。

of God present with the believers. I could not
help but feel people were giving expression to
some existential logic that in order to realise
one's self, or fulfil one's self, one walks with
God.

The word "Catholic" in Japanese is translated
using the character 公 (kō) meaning "public."
Kō in this sense does not mean "god" or
"supreme being," but rather "daily," or
"universal," some ordinary practice natural.
I think this expression also applies to the
Catholic Mass. Here the direction of the
vector is relative. With the French Revolution,
from which democracy is said to originate,
the vector was from citizens to rulers, and the
conduct of peoples' lives, and the meaning of
Catholic, can be thought to accord with this
trajectory.

There are people who think that the "quiet"
Japanese Mass is lacking in some way (some
foreign priests say they are all like funerals…).
For example, people from The Philippines.
In the church on Sado Island (off the west
coast of Japan) I saw them there singing and
dancing on the old tatami (straw mat) floor.
This shocked me a little, but I felt that they
probably participated in Mass more enjoyably
in their own country.

90

雲の切れ間から降りてくる光のフレアー。日本語では天孫降臨、英語では Angelstairs。
p.20 のガラスのむこう。
A FLARE FALLING THROUGH A BREAK IN THE CLOUDS. IN JAPANESE SUCH A
SIGHT IS SAID TO RECALL THE DESCENT TO EARTH OF THE GRANDSON OF THE
SUN GODDESS. IN ENGLISH IT IS KNOW AS ANGEL STAIRS. (THE OTHER SIDE OF
THE GLASS IN THE PHOTOGRAPH ON PAGE 20)

コーブ（CoBh）手前の小さな駅。ホームを絡ぐ跨線橋が優雅。
A SMALL RAILWAY STATION ON THE WAY TO COBH. THE STEEL
BRIDGE OVER THE RAILWAY LINE IS QUITE ELEGANT.

駐車禁止
アイルランドでは日曜日の午前中は駐車禁止がありません。どこにクルマを停めても
OK。それは教会のミサがあるから。街でも（特に田舎では）ほとんどの人々は自分の
車で教会を訪れます。駐車場はそんなに広くないのでどうしてもその辺りの道路に停め

Parking Prohibited
In Ireland there is no prohibition of parking on Sunday mornings. You
may park your car anywhere. This is said to be because of the many people
attending Masses. In both urban and rural areas most people travel to Mass
by car. Since the car parks beside churches are usually not very large, many
people park on the roadside near the church they attend. This is especially
true of elderly people (and many of those who attend church are elderly),
so there is a flood of cars parked around many churches. Just imagining, I
wonder if at some time the police did issue parking tickets to people parking
on the street while attending Mass, and then there were so many tickets to
be issued that the policeman himself was unable to attend Mass, and giving
up said "park wherever you want!" I wonder if such was the case.

河口とも干潟ともつかない湿地に架かる石橋。うしろは羊の丘。
A STONE BRIDGE OVER WATER THAT IS NEITHER A RIVER ESTUARY NOR
MARSH. BEYOND IS A HILLSIDE WITH SHEEP.

てしまいます。特に高齢者の場合（教会に来る人たちは高齢者が多い）その傾向が強いので教会とそのまわり
はまさに車の洪水になってしまいます。そこでこの先は想像ですが、はじめは警察もいっしょうけんめい取締っ
ていたのでしたが、反則キップを切っても切っても追いつかない、それと警官もミサに参加したい、等々の理
由で「え～い！　それならもうぜーんぶ自由にしてしまえ！」と、このようになったのではないでしょうか。

ミレーの晩鐘

絵画に関してはほとんど知らないけどミレーの晩鐘だけは以前から心に残っていて、このあいだ複製画を買
い求めました。場面はフランスの田園、刈り取りが終わった畑の中で2人の農夫（婦）が感謝の祈りをささげて
いるところです。光の醸し出す雰囲気から読み取れる時刻は夕刻の6時。足もとの農具のほかに村の教会が小
さく描かれています。鐘が響き渡る時、人々は手を休め一瞬の黙想に浸ります。
現在のアイルランドでも鐘の音がテレビやラジオから流れて来て、人々は同様に祈りのひと時を過ごします。時
を越えて行ない継がれる人の営みです。

Millet's The Angelus

I know little about famous paintings, but Jean-François Millet's The Angelus made a deep
impression on me many years ago., and recently I bought a copy. The setting is in rural
France; two people, a man and a woman, have stopped their work and bow their heads as
they pray. The atmosphere evoked by the light suggests that the time is around 6PM. Along
with the work tools at their feet, in the distance is a small image of the bell tower of the
village church. As the sound of the church bell echoes around them, people rest their hands,
and submerge in reflection for a few moments.
In Ireland today the sound of the Angelus Bell is still to be heard on radio and television, and
people pause for a few moments of prayer. This action transcends time and place.

むこうの海と丘
THE SEA AND THE LAND

修道院で夕食を共にしたクラーク神父様 (神奈川・藤沢教会で司牧、現在は本部の修道院でのんびり……) が、
「あした出発の前にお茶できるかな」
「すみません、きのうから申し上げているように明朝5時にはここを出ないと飛行機が……」
「それじゃ、3時ではどう?」
「……」
☆コロンバン会本部修道院 (p.58 ～ 59) はタラの丘に向いて建っています。写真の右方1～2キロメートルのところにタラの丘があります。天気がよければどちらからも見渡すことができます。

The night before returning home
I joined Fr Clarke at the evening meal in St Columban's Priests' Residence. Fr Clarke previously ministered at Fujisawa church in Kanagawa Prefecture, and is now enjoying retirement at St Columban's. When I asked "will I be able to have some tea before leaving tomorrow? As I mentioned yesterday, I will have to leave here at 5AM if I am to be at the airport in time for my flight." "How about 3AM" he replied. St Columban's is built facing the Hill of Tara (pages 58-59). The Hill of Tara is just a couple of kilometres distant, and is visible on the right side of the photograph. If the day is clear each can be seen from the other.

写真・文　伊藤　龍也

Photographs and text : Ito Tatsuya

1952年東京生まれ。写真家。古い建物や教会の撮
影、地元立川市や多摩地区の歴史と文化を写真で
記録する。「こころにのこしておきたいね」と感じて
もらえる内容と表現をこころがける。

Ito Tatsuya
Born in Tokyo in 1952. Freelance photographer.
Specialises in photographs of old buildings
and churches. Works compiling a cultural
and historical record in photographs for his
native Tachikawa City and the Tama area. "I
would like to cherish these impressions" is
the response he desires of those who savour
the contents of this book.

翻訳　ダニエル・ホーガン

Translation : Daniel Horgan

1955年アイルランドのコーク生まれ。カトリック司祭
で宣教会聖コロンバン会員です。1979-2008日本の力
トリック教会の宗教活動に携わった。　古来の伝統
を重んじる日本人はとても印象的でした。

Daniel Horgan
Born in Cork, Ireland in 1955. A Catholic
priest, and member of the Missionary
Society of St.Columban; worked in Japan
from 1979 until 2008. The manner in
which Japanese people honour their ancient
traditions made a deep impression on him.

本稿については次の方々にたいへんお世話になりました。　アイルランドの友人たち、　コロニー印刷スタッフの
方々、論創社森下社長と誉田氏 。ありがとうございました。

I wish to express my special thanks to the following people who provided me with advice
and support in compiling this book : My many Irish friends, The staff of Koroni Printing,
Mr. Morishita Director and Mr. Honda Editor of Ronsosha.

アイルランド　人のいとなみ

2020年11月5日　初版第1刷印刷
2020年11月10日　初版第1刷発行

写真・文　伊藤龍也

翻　訳　ダニエル・ホーガン

発 行 人　森下紀夫

発 行 所　論創社
東京都千代田区神田神保町2-23 北井ビル
tel. 03 (3264) 5254
fax. 03 (3264) 5232
web. http://www.ronso.co.jp/
振替口座　00160-1-155266

装幀・組版／社会福祉法人 コロニー印刷
印刷・製本／中央精版印刷
©2020　Ito Tatsuya

Printed in Japan
ISBN978-4-8460-1897-9
落丁・乱丁本はお取り替えいたします。

Ireland: People & Life

First Published in 2020 by Ronsosha
Kitai Bldg, Kandajinbocho 2-23,
Chiyoda-ku, Tokyo, Japan
Tel 03-3264-5254
http://www.ronso.co.jp

Photographs and text: Ito Tatsuya
Translation: Daniel Horgan
Publisher: Morishita Norio

Typeset by Colony Printing
Printed by Chuoseihan Printing
©2020　Ito Tatsuya

Printed in Japan
ISBN 978-4-8460-1897-9